Tlingit Design and Carving Manual

TLINGIT DESIGNS

The intent of this book is to provide some ideas or basis for
basic designs for the student of Tlingit design. Having been
interested in Northwest Coast Art for two decades, as a hobby
and later as a living, the author has experienced the frustra-
tion of having to find out the how, when, where, and why of the
designs. It is hoped that the follower of Northwest Coast
design will benefit from the material presented here.

Tlingit Design

Written and illustrated by Raymond E. Peck

Contributors:

Anthony Pope - photographs

Arnold Weimer - photographs

Robert Peck - halibut hook

Veita Jo Hampton - photographs

Jim Marks - designs (JM)

Wanda Culp - drawing

"Through the ages Northwest Coast Indian art remains one of the most beautiful and functional forms of traditional cultural art found anywhere. Symmetry, smooth flowing lines, complimentary colors, sharp detail and elusive, mystical symbolism all contribute to the beauty of totemic designs."

 **Superior** PUBLISHING COMPANY

SEATTLE, WASHINGTON

Library of Congress Cataloging in Publication Data

Peck, Raymond E
    Tlingit designs and carving manual.

    1. Tlingit Indians--Wood-carving. 2. Indians
of North America--Alaska--Wood-carving. I. Title.
E99.T6R38   736'.4   78-11887
ISBN 0-87564-861-4 PBK
ISBN 0-87564-862-2 H.B.

FIRST EDITION

PRINTED IN THE UNITED STATES OF AMERICA

This book is dedicated to Doreen and Renee
for they and their generation will create the
art for the future, and to the Juneau-Douglas
School District Indian Studies Program, Len
Sevdy, Director, for its continuing efforts
to revive Indian arts, language and dancing
for the children.

CONTENTS

SECTION 1:   "Lovebirds"

SECTION 2:   Raven and Subclans

       Raven
       Beaver
       Dog Salmon
       Frog
       Seagull

SECTION 3:   Eagle and Subclans

       Eagle
       Bear
       Killerwhale
       Wolf
       Thunderbird

SECTION 4:   Combination of Designs

SECTION 5:   Tlingit (the man)

SECTION 6:   Elements

       eye, eyebrow
       nose
       mouth, teeth and tongue
       ear
       wing
       claws, paws, feet and hands
       tails (bird, fish, animal)

SECTION 7:   Miscellaneous

S E C T I O N   1

"LOVEBIRDS"

The designation "lovebirds" is not a traditional name in the Tlingit
culture. The term is a fairly recent adaptation of the <u>custom</u> of the
Tlingits. A Tlingit being either Raven or Eagle clan (moiety) must marry
the opposite clan. Thus, the Eagle and Raven have become shown side by
side on an equal basis. When designing an Eagle-Raven motif be sure to
keep them balanced in all aspects so as not to offend anyone belonging
to either clan, as much pride is taken in a Tlingit's ancestry.

EAGLE AND RAVEN

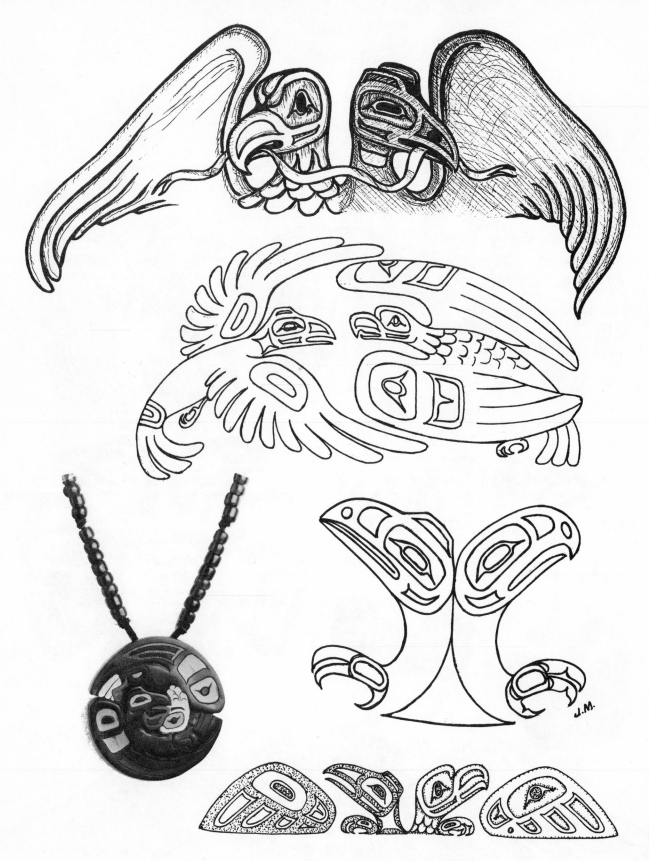

EAGLE AND RAVEN

SECTION 2

RAVEN AND SUBCLANS

The Raven is the most colorful of characters, being a sly trickster with supernatural powers. Many stories center around the Raven and his doings, including the creation of daylight and rivers. For this reason, more space is dedicated to the Raven.

Subclans under the Raven (in alphabetical order so as not to denote importance) are: Beaver, Coho Salmon, Crane, Crow, Dog Salmon, Frog, Land Otter, Mosquito, Sea Lion, Sea Pigeon (Seagull), Snail, Sockeye Salmon, Weasel, Whale, Wood Worm, Wolverine.

Not all subclans under the Raven are listed here and not all are illustrated.

RAVEN

Red

Blue-green

RAVEN

RAVEN

RAVEN

Red

Blue-green

BEAVER

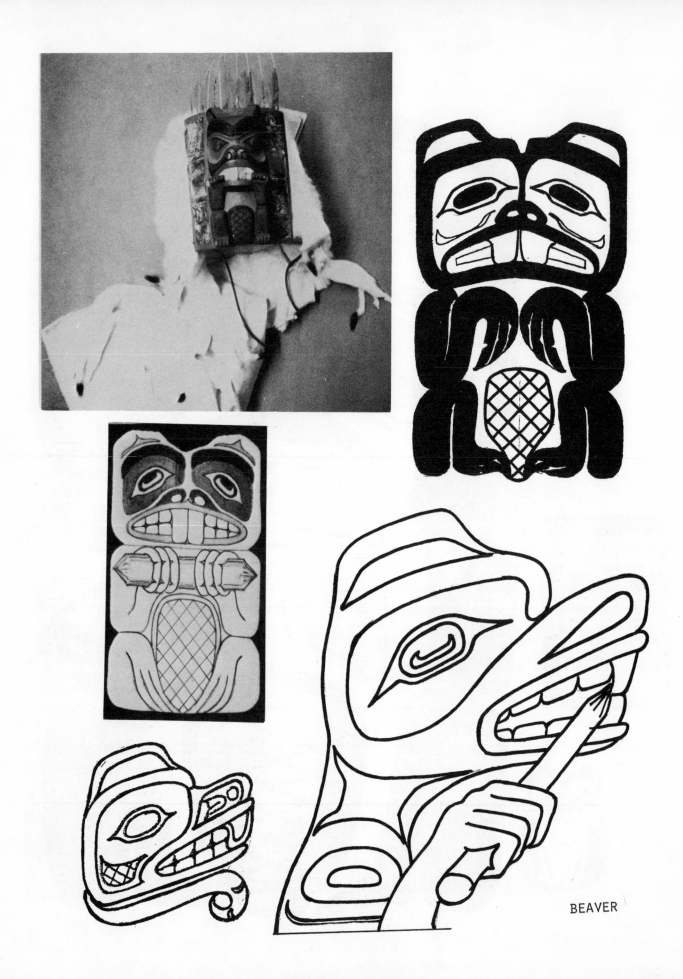

BEAVER

SALMON

HALIBUT

FROG

Red

Blue-green

FROG

LM

SEAGULL

Red

Blue-green

SECTION 3

EAGLE AND SUBCLANS

The Eagle represents the other moiety of the Tlingit Tribe which at one time was the Wolf. The Tlingits are matrilinial. A child becomes the same clan as the mother. An Eagle or Raven will have another subclan under the main clan, for example: Raven/Frog, Eagle/Killerwhale, as a crest.

In alphabetical order, <u>some</u> of the subclans or phratries under Eagle are: Bear, Glacier, Halibut, Killerwhale, Moon, Murrelet, Porpoise, Seal, Shark, Thunderbird, White Raven, Wolf.

Only some of the subclans under the Eagle have been illustrated.

 Red

 Blue-green

EAGLE

BEAR

 Red   Blue-green

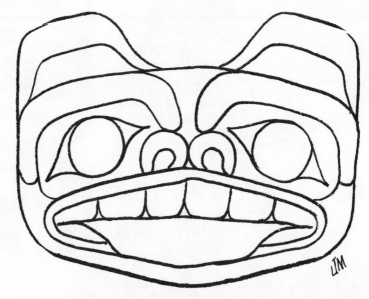

BEAR

The Carving Shop

INDIAN CARVINGS
PAINTINGS
DEMONSTRATIONS

KILLERWHALE

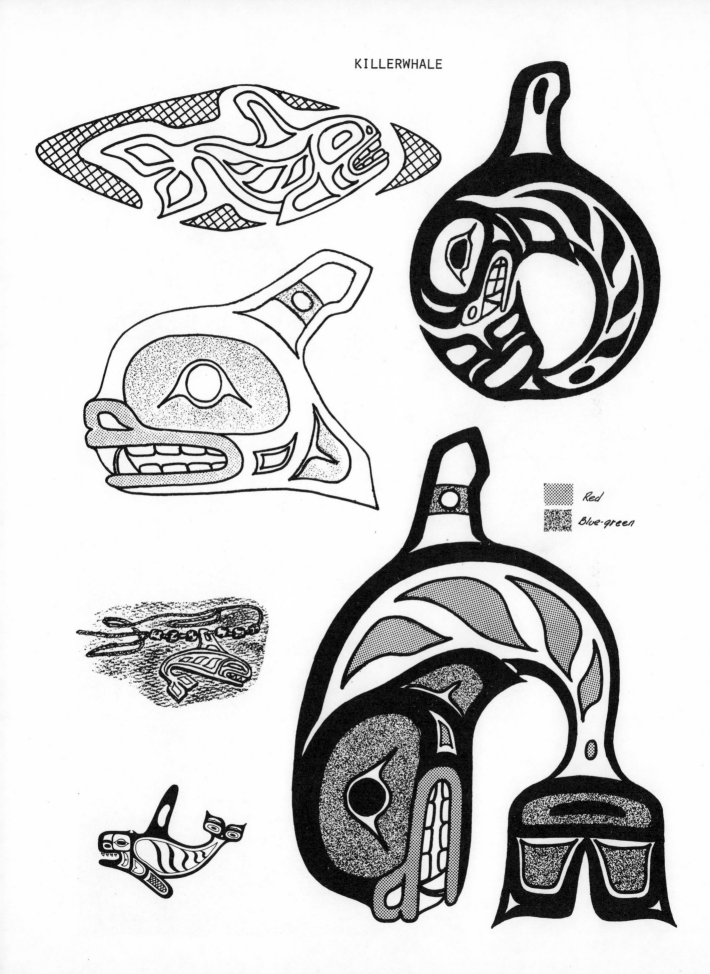

Red

Blue-green

KILLERWHALE

WOLF

Red

Blue-green

WOLF

THUNDERBIRD

:::: Red

:::: Blue-green

S E C T I O N 4

COMBINATION OF DESIGNS

As previously mentioned, a Tlingit's crest consists of more than one character, for example: Eagle/Bear, Raven/Beaver. Also, in depicting legends the artist will show the important characters as on a totem pole or house panel. Only a few of these combined designs are shown here.

Before working on a crest that does not belong to you, permission must be obtained from a leader of the clan who owns the crest you intend to use.

COMBINATION

STRONGMAN

SPIRITS

RAVEN-BEAVER

SECTION 5

TLINGIT (THE MAN)

The designs of the Tlingit were similar in appearance but yet the style varied from artist to artist as well as village to village. Sometimes an artifact could be recognized as having been done by a certain individual provided he was widely known.

A human figure, when depicted by an artist, varied from realistic to a hardly recognizable stylized form.

The appearance of the human may depend upon the circumstances surrounding it. The figure may represent a human or animal spirit, a changeable, supernatural character, or an actual person. To depict a story or legend you must know it thoroughly and if it belongs to a certain clan you must get their consent to use it.

OWL WOMAN

KUSHDAKA

SALMON BOY

TLINGIT

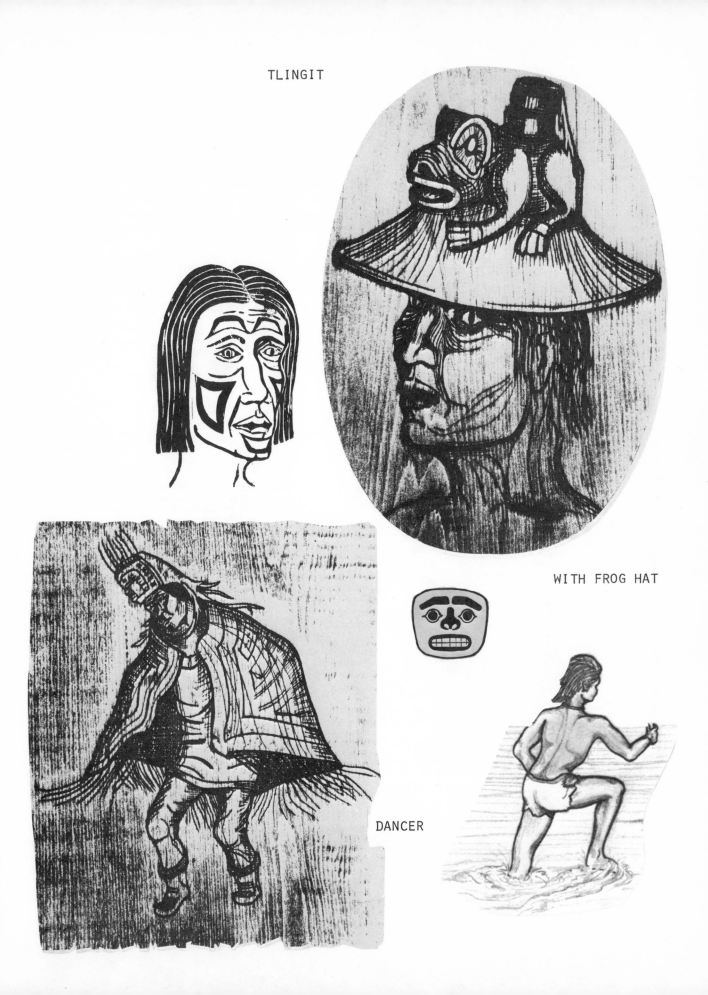

WITH FROG HAT

DANCER

S E C T I O N 6

ELEMENTS

Most of the Tlingit designs include certain elements which contribute to
the overall design.

The eye is probably the most common and important element of the total
design. The eye represents "action" or "life" and is shown on major
joints of the body as well as on the head. Some of the various styles
of eyes are shown below. A large rounded eye will be found in a large
rectangular space, a narrow eye for a narrower area.

The eye must conform to the shape of the head as well as the eye and eye
socket.

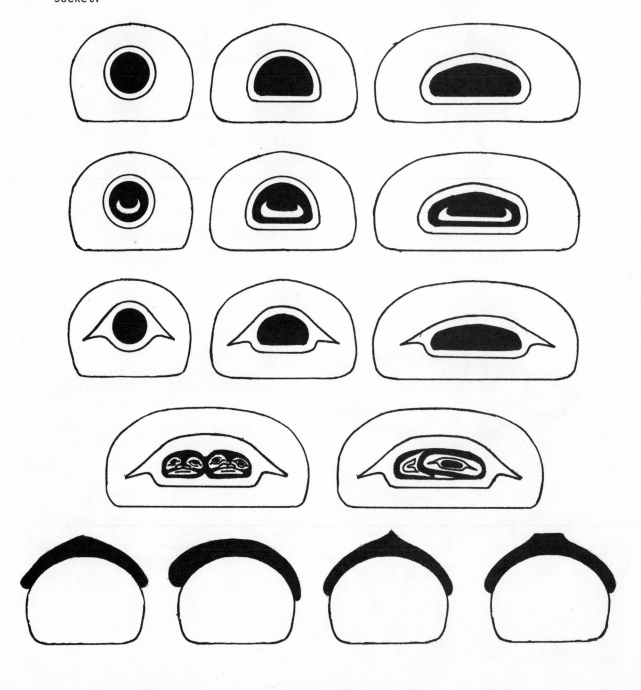

There are many different types of noses and nostrils. <u>Some</u> of them are shown here. Remember that the nose should be smooth flowing, fit the space and fit the character.

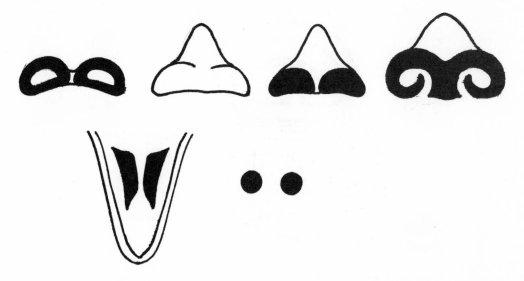

A lot of expression can be shown in the mouth, teeth and tongue (when applicable). Fierceness, passiveness or just a recognizable quality is shown with the mouth. Many times this element can be the difference between a good, well-balanced design or a not-so-good design.

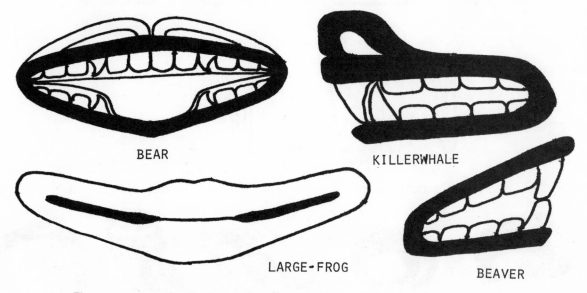

BEAR

KILLERWHALE

LARGE-FROG

BEAVER

The ear comes in various shapes and sizes depending upon the space to be filled and somewhat to the actual shape of the animal's **ear**. A few are illustrated here.

WOLF BEAR-BEAVER-RAVEN

The wing may be divided into major parts, the upper solid area and the lower wing feathers.

UPPER WING
LOWER WING

The upper wing usually has an eye with other space fillers. The eyes were covered earlier and some of the space fillers are shown below.

Some of the lower wing feather-fillers are shown here.

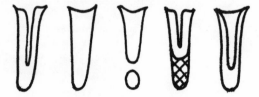

Claws, paws, feet and hands.

BIRDS FROG REAR PAW FRONT PAW

TAILS

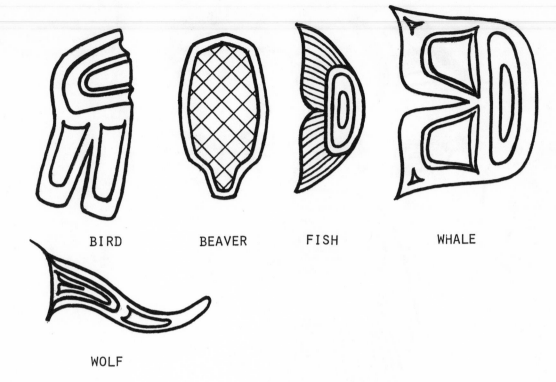

BIRD   BEAVER   FISH   WHALE

WOLF

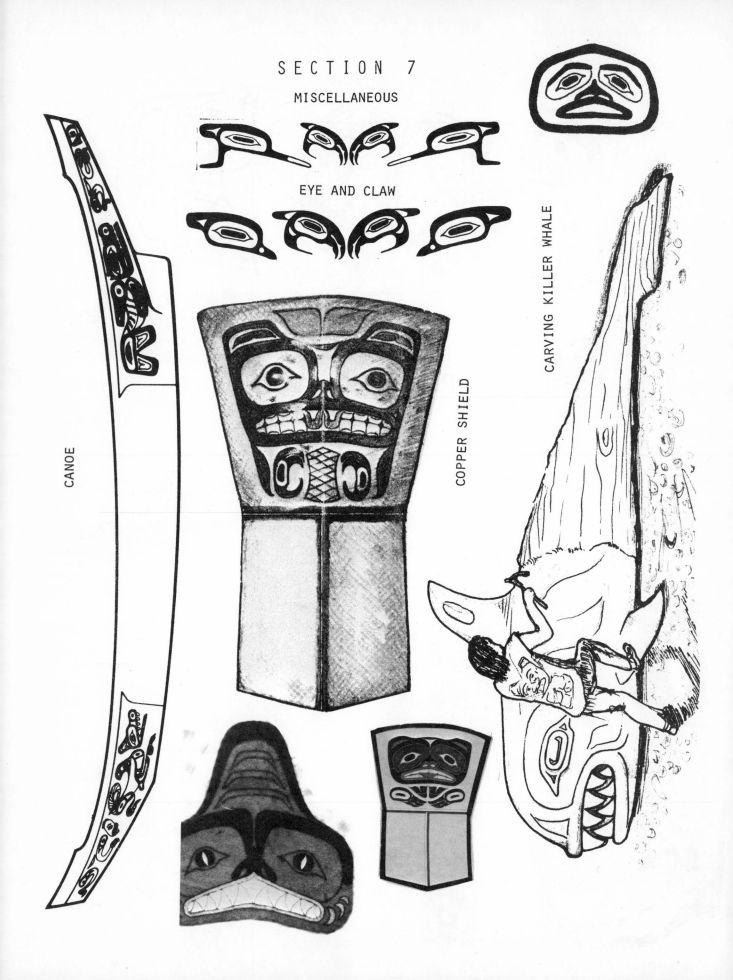

SECTION 7

MISCELLANEOUS

EYE AND CLAW

CANOE

COPPER SHIELD

CARVING KILLER WHALE

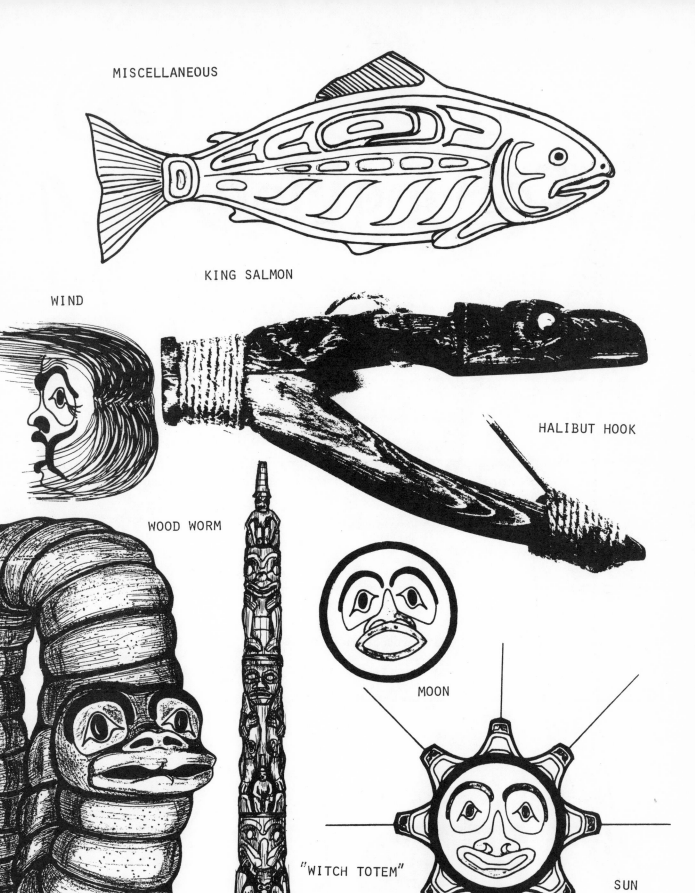

MISCELLANEOUS

KING SALMON

WIND

HALIBUT HOOK

WOOD WORM

MOON

"WITCH TOTEM"

SUN

Carving Manual

Written and Illustrated by Raymond E. Peck

Front and back cover photos by Anthony Pope

"Totems weren't carved to hold their stories in secret, but to commemorate an event and remind the Tlingit of his rich heritage."

CONTENTS

SECTION 1   Northwest Coast Indians

SECTION 2   Tools

SECTION 3   Use of Tools

SECTION 4   Making Tools

SECTION 5   Care of Tools

SECTION 6   Selecting Wood

SECTION 7   Roughing Out

SECTION 8   Sketching the Design

SECTION 9   Intermediate Carving

SECTION 10   Finishing Touches

SECTION 11   Conclusion

S E C T I O N   1

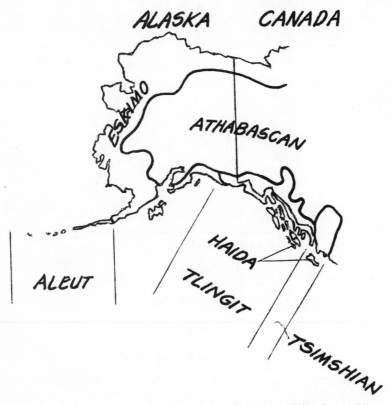

NORTHWEST COAST INDIANS

ALASKA   CANADA

ESKIMO

ATHABASCAN

HAIDA

TLINGIT

ALEUT

TSIMSHIAN

    This book is concerned primarily with the Tlingit Indians and
their art. The styles and appearance of the art work of various tribes
are distinguishable although some designs were borrowed or traded and
the origin of some artifacts is not known. As shown on the preceding
map, the Tlingit Indians dominated most of S.E. Alaska. The Tlingit,
Tsimpsian, Haida and Kwakiutl Indians all had very stylized designs
of birds, animals and fish which represented various clans or legends.
In some cases these designs represented spirits. Totem poles had
nothing to do with religion and were not worshiped. The Tlingit,
when compared with the other tribes mentioned, had the most recognizable or basic designs. The Tsimpsian Indians embelished their carvings
with many small, detailed figures. The Haida, who have most developed
the art of carving, have smooth flowing, rounded figures which are
harder to interpret than the prior two groups mentioned. Kwakiutl art
is bold to the point of being grotesque having sharp detail and con-
trast in form and color.

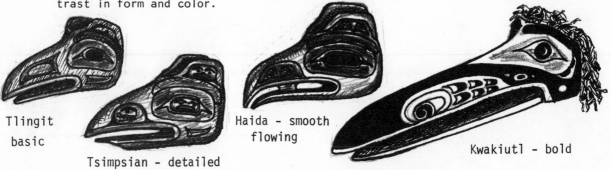

Tlingit
basic

Tsimpsian - detailed

Haida - smooth
flowing

Kwakiutl - bold

These tribes all used three basic colors as accents and very sparingly as several materials had to be gathered and these mixed to obtain one color. The colors used were black (most common), red and bluegreen, usually evenly balanced. White was also sometimes used.

A person could only use the designs of the clan to which he belonged or he may use another design with permission from the owner. Recognized artists of a different clan could be commissioned by wealthy leaders to do art works for the leaders. Totem poles depicted a clan's lineage or told a story which belonged to a family or clan.

House posts (used to hold up roof beams), large panels, and house fronts all told stories or reflected the owner's emblem or clan. Other carved items included canoes, food dishes, storage boxes, large spoons, paddles, masks, dance staffs, halibut hooks, war or fish clubs and hats or helments and headdresses.

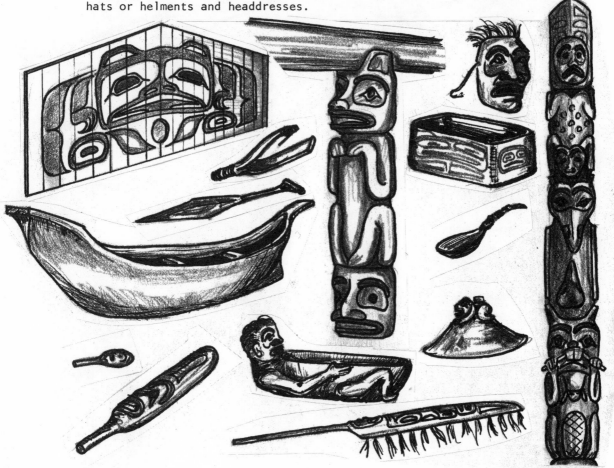

carved Tlingit items

The Tlingit tribe was divided into two major clans. The Eagle and the Raven. These two clans were further divided into subclans. Thus a person could have as an emblem or crest a Raven with a beaver under it. These emblems could be compared to the European Coats of Arms.

Some representative animal crests come into being when one clan or village grew too large, and some would separate and migrate to another area. Tlingits were food gatherers and hunter-fishermen, and this made it difficult to support large groups in one area. During their travels a sign or happening having to do with a certain animal was experienced.

Raven and <u>some</u> of its sub-clans.

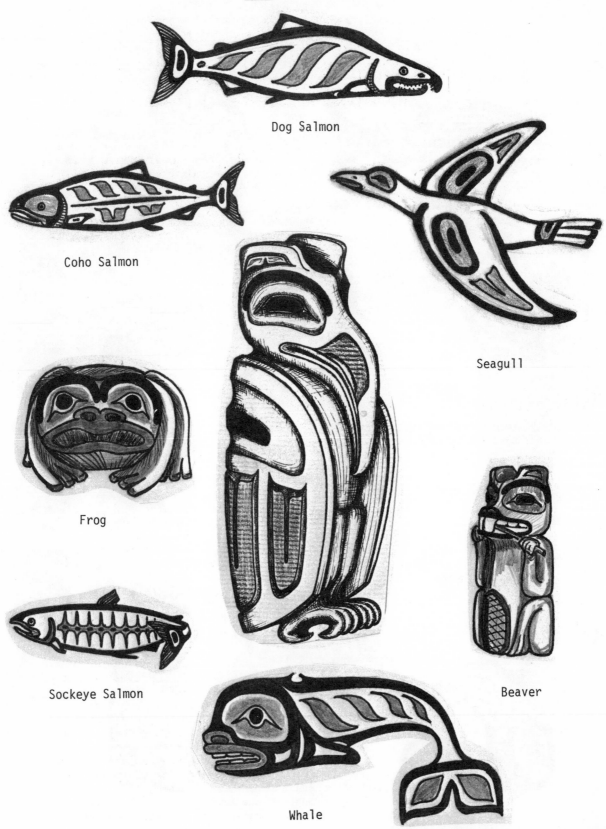

Dog Salmon

Coho Salmon

Seagull

Frog

Beaver

Sockeye Salmon

Whale

Eagle and <u>some</u> of its sub-clans.

Halibut

Thunderbird

Wolf

Shark

Killer whale

Bear

Eagle/bear crest   Raven/beaver crest

This animal might then be picked to represent their clan, especially if
this animal had good or fierce qualities.

     After food gathering and storing seasons the Tlingits had much time
in the winter months for ceremonies and preparing clothing and carving.
The availability of good carving wood made it possible to develop carving
to a high degree.

SECTION 2

TOOLS

Before contact with early explorers the Northwest Coast Indians used sharp stone, bone, antler, shell and teeth for knife cutting edges. Explorers and traders brought about the availability of iron for use as knife blades.

Two main types of knives are used for carving, one is the straight blade knife which has a flat underside and beveled edge on the top and

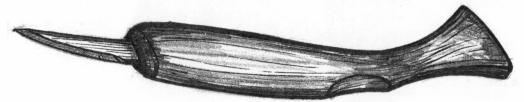

Straight-blade right handed knife

the other is the curved blade knife with a flat bottom, beveled edges

Curved-blade right handed knife

on top and curved on top. The handles of the knives are just as important as the blades. The handle should fit in your hand comfortably,
if not you will tire quickly, get blisters after a long period of
carving and the quality of your work will suffer. The handles are
usually of hardwood, curved up and out from your palm. If your blade

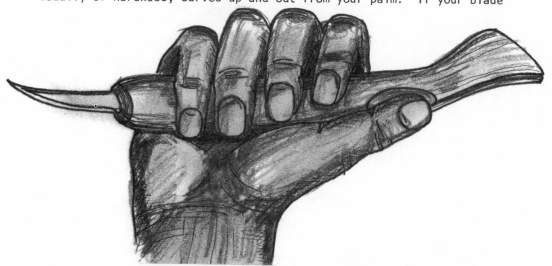

Holding knife

is to be strapped on by wire or twine the strapping material should be
inset or inlaid into the handle so that the whole handle is smooth (has

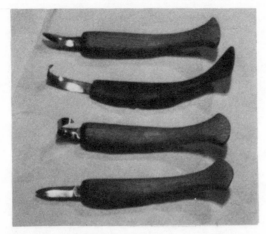

Wood handles

no obstructions) down to the blade. Bone or antler handles may be used
providing a good fit can be obtained.

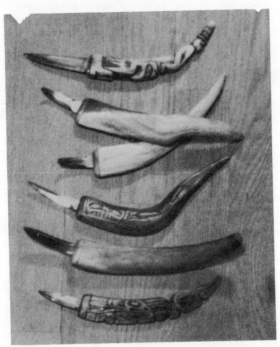

Antler handles

The adz is an important tool used for roughing out carvings or
applying a finished textured effect to a house plank, totem pole or

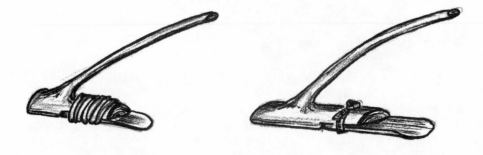

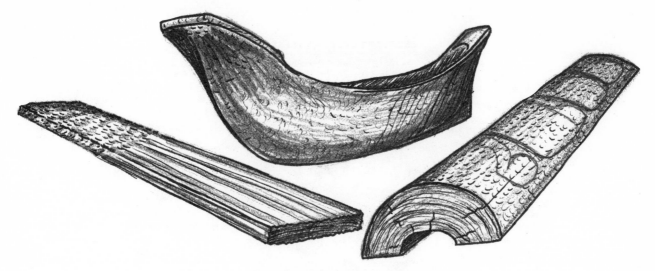

the adz and uses

canoe. A definate need for chisels arises in carving for getting into
hard-to-get-at places. Saws are also valuable at times to get chunks of

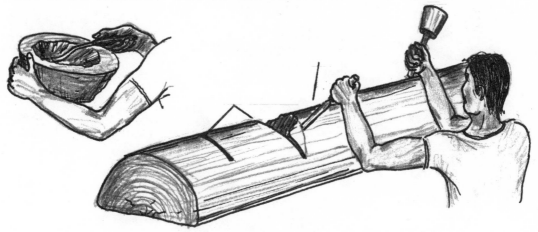

wood out of an area. If you are faced with getting your own raw wood,
as opposed to commercial lumber, you may have a need for splitting
wedges. Some other tools which may come in handy in your carving are
draw knives and hand planes.

    Remember to keep your tool collection to a minimum and add tools
as you need them. Do not begin by buying a lot of tools you think
you'll need and ending up not using most of them.

S E C T I O N   3

USE OF TOOLS

Special tools were developed centuries ago for certain types of
carving. These same styles of knives and adzes are still being made by
hand and used today along with modern commercial tools.

Care must be taken in handling any knife and especially a carving
knife as these must be kept very sharp.

The straight blade knife is used for planing and also for making

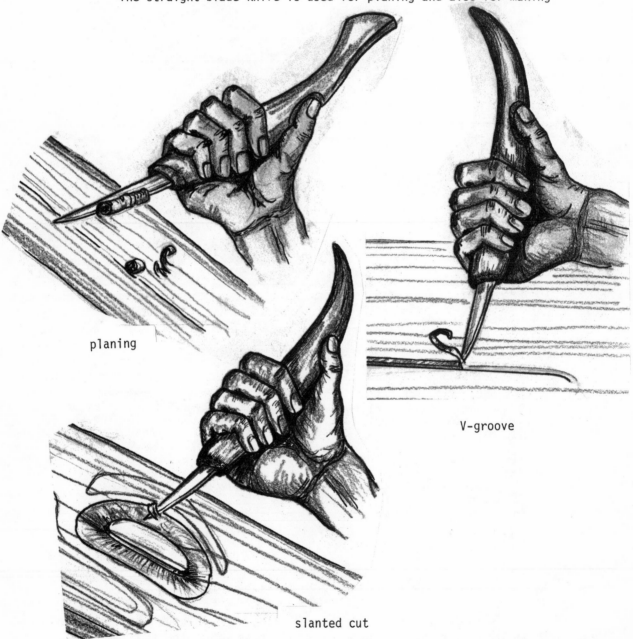

planing

V-groove

slanted cut

V-grooves or slanted cuts. The straight blade knife if the top is
rounded and not beveled can be pushed away with the use of your thumb.

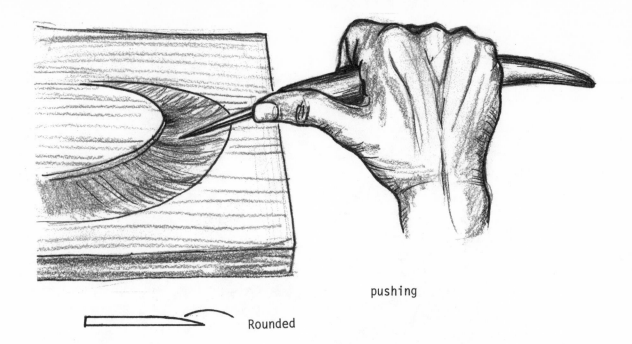

pushing

Rounded

Another tool which might be classified as a straight blade knife are the inexpensive little hobby-craft type knives which can be used for fine detail. The angle of the tip of the blade will determine the ease of cutting corners or curves without leaving jagged tracks.

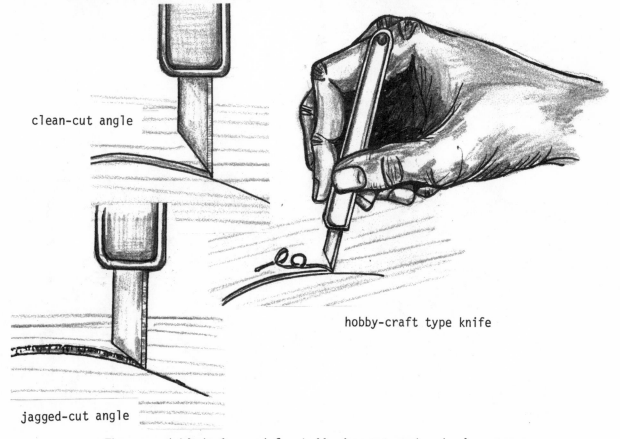

clean-cut angle

hobby-craft type knife

jagged-cut angle

The curved blade is used for hollowing out masks, bowls, spoons, rattles, etc. The curved blade, if both edges are sharp, can be pushed

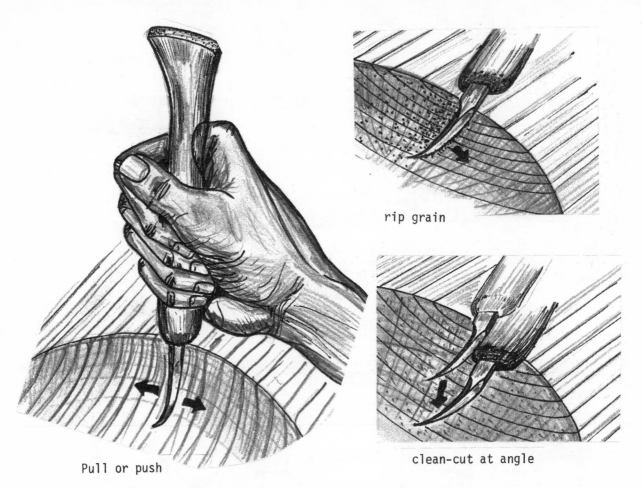

rip grain

clean-cut at angle

Pull or push

or pulled to cut with the grain or at an angle to the grain. At times
cutting directly across the grains will tend to bunch them up and leave
holes. Usually sliding your blade in a different direction over these
areas will result in a smoother cut.

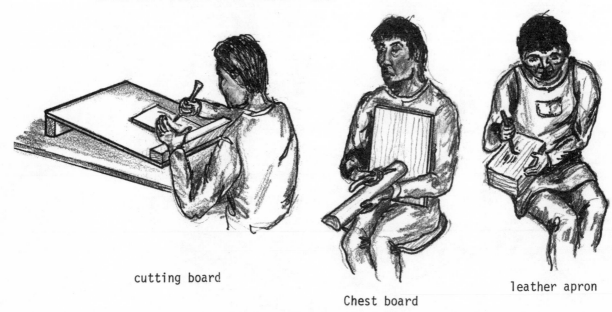

cutting board

Chest board

leather apron

Some protective devices, shown here, can be used to insure against
cutting yourself.

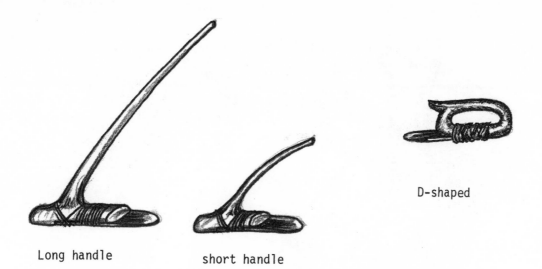

D-shaped

Long handle   short handle

Handling the adz requires developing a special skill but when this skill is attained you'll have an invaluable tool. Since this tool is used in a hacking motion, downward and towards you, care must be taken in not putting too much force in your swing and also keeping yourself out of the way.

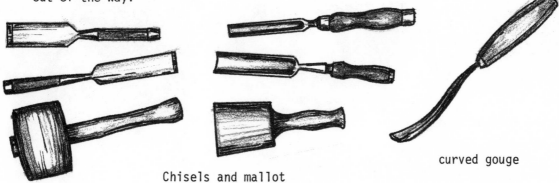

curved gouge

Chisels and mallot

Using straight chisels with a mallot presents no problem as both your hands are out of the way. Using gouges or curved chisels however,

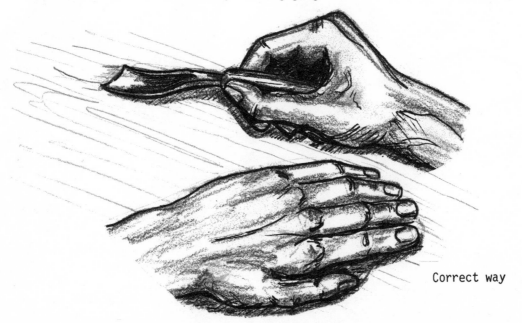

Correct way

Incorrect way

can be dangerous. Usually you will push on the gouge while holding the
wood down with your other palm. Be sure your holding hand is not in
the path of the gouge or use clamps to hold your work in place.

SECTION 4

MAKING TOOLS

Knife blades were always made of the best available material so it stands to reason that now tool steel is widely used. The tool steel can be obtained either in commercial sheet form about 1/16" thick by ordering or it can be obtained from old files, scrap heavy duty hacksaw blades or other cutting material. The shapes of the blades (covered in Chapter II) depends on your own needs and preferences.

The best all-around blade has two edges and tapered towards the middle for cutting in both directions and with a slight curve at the tip. The blade is cut out roughly with a hacksaw then shaped with a

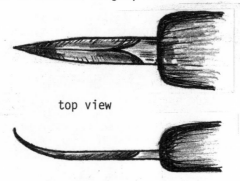

top view

side view

grinder. While grinding keep the blade cooled off by occassionally dipping in water. The cutting edge is then filed smooth. If the tip is

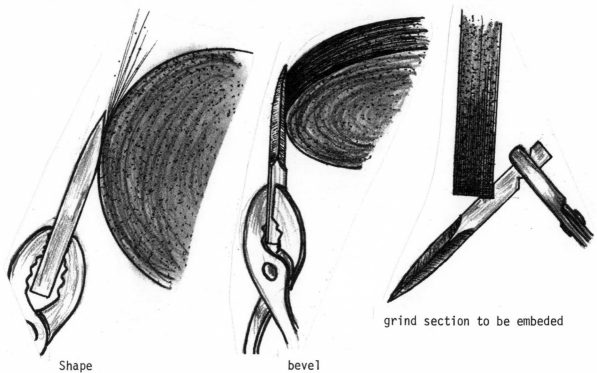

Shape

bevel

grind section to be embeded

to be bent it will have to be heated slightly and hammered over a curved object.

Bending blade

    After bending is accomplished or if the blade is to be flat you
are ready to harden and temper. Hardening of tool steel can be accom-
plished by heating to cherry-red and quickly putting into a can of
water or oil until cool. The hardening and tempering process will help
to keep a sharpe edge longer. To temper polish the blade then heat
until purple around 500 F and then cool slowly. Hardening metal is a
science in itself and only the basic process will be mentioned here.

    The handle should fit your hand perfectly. The block of wood
from which it is to be shaped should be a least 1 1/2'' x 2'' x 6''
medium or hard wood. The basic shape can be cut out on a ban saw.

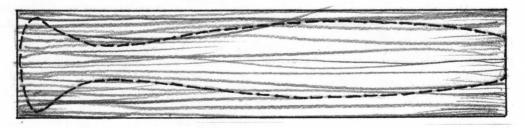

Top view

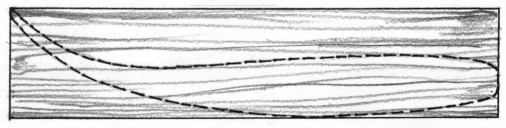

side view

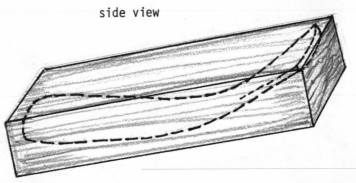

A wood rasp may then be used to round off the corners. The blade is
set near to the botton of the handle so the wood will either be dug

Good fit

out from the end or the bottom of the handle will be cut out the entire

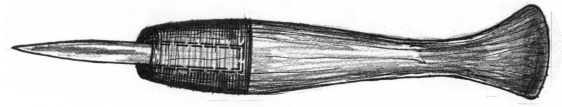

Top view - inlay or inset blade

length of the blade stem to be inset. Some type of high strength epoxy
should be used and if the handle was just cut for the blade to be inlaid,
then wire or twine should be wound around it also.

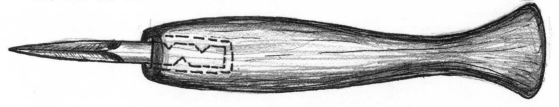

Bottom view - blade inlay with wire
(notch wood so that twine or wire will end up same perimeter)

The same process can be used with bone or antler handles. When
gouging out the end of the bone or antler handle the entire soft portion
or porous material should be removed to the hard outer shell as deep as
the blade is to be inset. A thin section can be cut off before digging

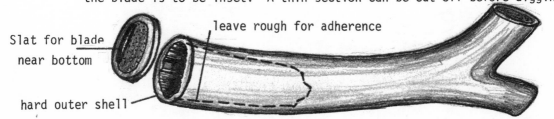

leave rough for adherence

Slat for blade
near bottom

hard outer shell

out the porous material to be used to cover the epoxy. A slot must be
cut for the blade at the desired location.

The adz is available commercially in various types such as flat,

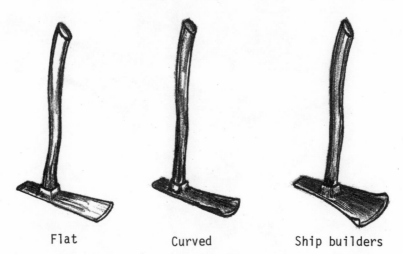

Flat   Curved   Ship builders

curved and shipbuilders. The hand made adz will be suited to your par-
ticular needs. The process for hardening is the same as for the knife

Chisel

Scrap steel

Chisel with ivory handle

blades. A large, heavy blade must be used for roughing out whereas a
small blade will be used for more refined work. The handle should be
in proportion to your blade. The best handle is a hardwood branch,

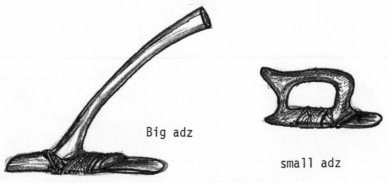

Big adz

small adz

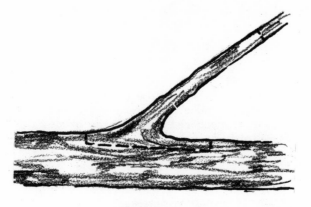

Branch

such as alder. The blade is then attached to the handle usually by
wire.

SECTION 5

CARE OF TOOLS

Using a dull tool will make twice as much work for you and the quality of your work will suffer. You will need coarse and medium sharpening stones to get a good edge on a newly made knife, but after that process all that is required are several grades of fine sharpening stones, fine emery cloth, leather.

In sharpening the straight blade the blade has to be laid flat on the stone and pushed in a circular motion. When sharpening the

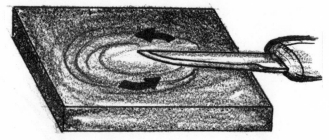

curved blade you must keep the bottom side flat against the stone even at the tip. Move in circular motion while moving towards tip. When

sharpening your adz, hold the adz upside down and slide the sharpening stone away from you at the same angle as the bevel. After stone

sharpening, your blade will have a little burm on the edge which will have to be removed. To remove the burm you can use fine emery cloth

from the top towards the edge. Then polish both top and bottom with leather. A round object or your finger wrapped with emery cloth or

leather will have to be used on the top side of the curved blade. The
blade should cut through wood like you were cutting butter. After a
good edge is obtained just touch up with emery cloth often to keep
the blade sharp.

Being careful, cannot be stressed enough especially while sharpening your carving tools as you are handling your tools in a different
manner than when you are carving.

SECTION 6

SELECTING WOOD

The Tlingit carvers of the past were very knowledgeable in the properties of the many types of wood which they carved. Strength, size, weight and availability were important in the selection of the wood to be carved. Some of the types of wood preferred by the author are yellow cedar, red cedar, red wood, alder and sugar pine. Yellow cedar is a close grained, light colored wood. Yellow cedar has a nice but acidy smell and is easy to work if a piece with straight grain is available. Some of this type wood is very hard. If the piece of cedar is damp it must be dried out slowly or cracks or "checks" will appear.

Red cedar is fairly soft with widely spaced big grain and is very light in weight. This wood tends to splinter easily. Red cedar doesn't rot as fast as other wood and was the type most used for totem poles.

Red wood is much the same as red cedar although some pieces of it seem to carve better.

Alder is good carving wood and is easily carved if kept damp. When completely dry, alder becomes very hard.

Sugar pine is very soft but it has large grain and tends to splinter.

In a cross section of a log, the center or heart doesn't shrink as it dries as does the surrounding wood which causes cracks and is a good reason for either splitting the log down the middle or cutting the center out of the log.

SECTION 7

ROUGHING OUT

The use of power tools is primarily up to the conscience of the artist. In other words modern society may dictate, that in order to make a descent living an artist will have to produce art works in the fastest way possible or to mass produce art. The old-time artist (where he would always adapt to improvements in materials or tools) probably would choose to create his art by hand or simple tools rather than by convenience. It is strictly up to the person, to either be an artist or machinest!

In wood sculpture different planes exist such as panel carvings (two dimensional) and totem poles (three dimensional). In roughing out a three dimensional carving simple rough sketches or guide lines must be made which will disappear with continued carving making it

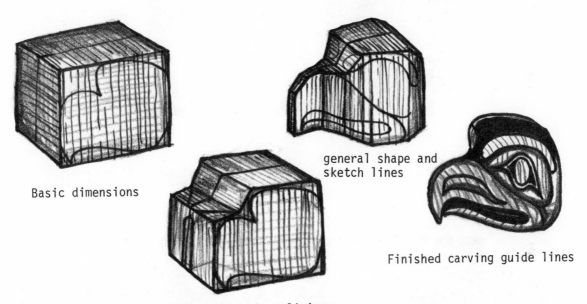

Basic dimensions

Rough cuts and preliminary
guide lines

general shape and
sketch lines

Finished carving guide lines

necessary to make new guide lines all the time. Unlike other sculptural mediums wood cannot be molded into shape!

SECTION 8

SKETCHING THE DESIGN

Any good carving or artistic creation must develop from a good
idea to begin with. Very few beautiful creations are made by chance.
In Northwest Coast Indian Art, you will find predominent design features
which will enable you to begin shaping your design and going to refined design features as you develop your carving.

Trace design

There are short cuts used by old time carvers to develop their
carvings. Most Northwest Coast Art is symmetrical so that patterns
can be made of one side and flipped over to make the other half. If
you make a drawing on paper with pencil go over the lines on the back
of the paper. When you trace this on wood you'll have a pencil-lead
drawing on the wood. A posterboard cutout (as shown) is a simple

cut out

method. The connecting parts have lines drawn through them. A third method is to draw your design then make pencil holes. After making points on the wood through the paper remove the design and connect all the points.

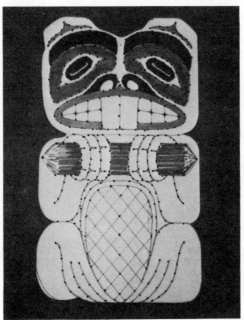

pencil-hole method

A method of measuring with a pencil is using your 3rd finger as a guide and making your line on one side of the object and without

Finger guide

changing position of your finger make the mark on the opposite side. Another way of accomplishing the same thing, especially if the distance is too great to use the first method, is to use a strip of paper or cardboard and make a mark on the strip where the opposite measurement will be.

S E C T I O N   9

INTERMEDIATE CARVING

As your carving progresses and the carving becomes finer you will start using finer knives. Some hobby-craft type knives as mentioned previously will be handy at this time. A carving knife with a blade of say 2" may end up, after many years of carving and sharpening, a little stub. These still can be used for fine detailed carving.

The beginning sketches are now the basic carving and your final sketching can be done. Use light pencil lines, one of the mistakes I've often made was using a soft lead pencil or marking pen and after making many changes and corrections had to sand off or carve away all the black marks. I've known some excellent carvers whose art products became so well done and balanced that gift shops would accuse the person of using machines to reproduce the objects and attempted to lower the purchase price of them. Most beginning carvers won't have this problem for awhile.

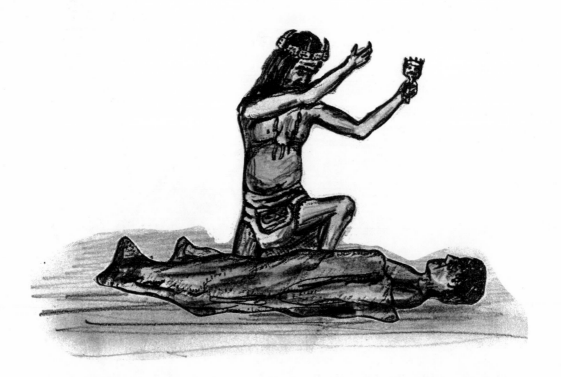

FINISHING TOUCHES

An easy trap to fall into is overdoing an already finished object or just not knowing when to stop. In most Northwest Coast Art
its the simplicity rather than the over doing of an object that made
the difference between a collector's item or a "tourist" trade piece.

One important skill to develop is getting a hollowed out object,
such as a mask, bowl, model canoe etc., to the right thickness so as
to not look bulky and yet not loose it's strength.

A high-school shop teacher once told me "you can keep cutting
wood off but you can't put it back." Also a friend of mine had
carved a mask so thin that in certain spots you could see light
through the wood. Developing a feel for thickness will become a
real asset.

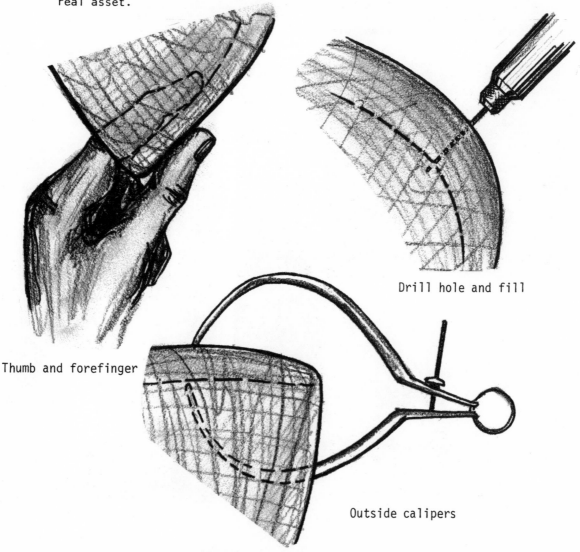

Drill hole and fill

Thumb and forefinger

Outside calipers

One of the best carvers I knew could get his carving smoother
with a knife than if he'd used fine sandpaper. However, years and
years of experience were necessary. Sometimes a chipped effect is
preferred to that of a sandpaper smooth look. Some carvers only

use water and a scrub brush to smooth out their carvings.

Several types of finishes are available to the carver. Some of these are staining, varnishing, and painting. At times the need arises to make an object look old or authentic and as your experience broadens you'll be able to prepare your own synthetic aging process. Some that I've learned of are using water poured through charcoal, and burying in damp soil for a length of time. There is however a commercial liquid application specifically for an aged appearance.

Other decorative materials would include pieces of copper shaped to fit the contours of masks and rattles. Usually used for eyes, eyebrows, lips, ear-outlines and other accents. Use copper brads to attach these pieces.

Abalone shell is a popular material which has to be inlayed. Care must be taken when working this very hard material as the dust is very toxic.

Some other decorative accents are small shell for teeth, some types of feathers, human hair, fur, sea-lion whiskers and leather.

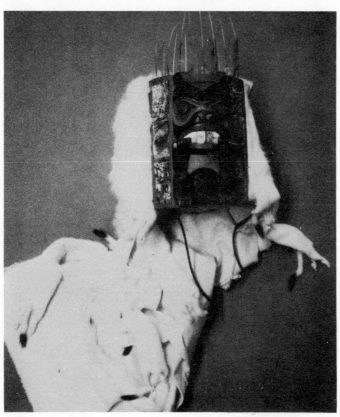

Paint, abalone shell, Sea Lion wiskers
feathers, fur

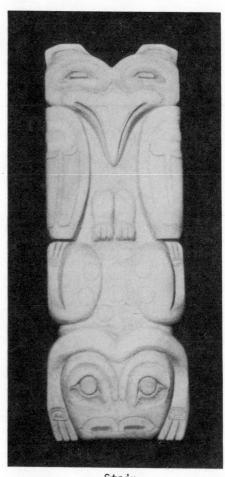

Stain

Keep in mind that you shouldn't overdo your art piece. A good rule to follow is to not use more than two or three types of accent materials on one piece of artwork.

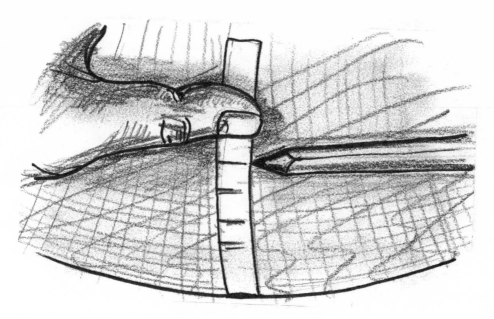

paper strip measurement

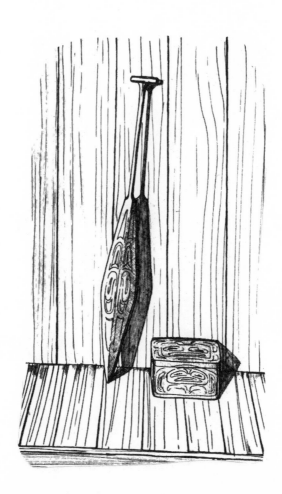

Paint and hair

Paint, copper and fur

S E C T I O N 11

CONCLUSION

It is hoped that some insight into the Tlingit culture and the reason for designs had been acquired plus further understanding of the making and use of carving tools. One of the most important steps in beginning to carve is to stop thinking about it and just "get started"!

notes